DARKEST DAWN

AN INSPIRATIONAL STORY BASED ON TRUE EVENTS

BONNY BROOKES

Cover Design: Bonny Brookes

Cover Photograph: Bonny Brookes

Copyright © 2013 Bonny Brookes

ISBN 0-9661342-2-2

DEDICATION

Life is a journey.
The decisions we make determine the roads we travel.

Dedicated to Nick and Mew.
I'm glad we traveled the same road, if only for awhile.

CONTENTS

ACKNOWLEDGMENTS

Thank you to Mikaela, Rhys, Jane, Nick, Mike, Danielle and Sandra. Without you, your encouragement, support and love this book might never have been. Thank you all.

1
RICHARD

The bathroom door opened as Linda walked out, leaned against the jamb and looked down at the small white cube she held in her hand. Dressed in sweats, she looked more like a teenage girl than the thirty-year-old woman she was.

Sweetie slept curled up on the couch. She walked over to him and sat down, careful not to drop the small white cube. Stroking the cat, she whispered, "Sweetie, wake up!" In answer, the cat opened one eye, looked up at her, then slowly stretched his large body. "Sweetie, look at this!" she said holding the cube under his nose. "It's a plus sign!"

The cat sniffed the cube then climbed onto her lap and closed his eyes to return to his dreams. Linda remained seated with the cat on her lap and petted his thick coat of white fur while she explained what she held. "I guess you don't understand. How could you? I understand it, but I don't even know what I'm feeling." She looked at the cube she held in her hand. "I'm pregnant. That makes me feel excited, surprised, elated, shocked, happy, yet mixed up . . . ," she swallowed the lump in her throat, "and scared."

Linda nibbled on her bottom lip. "I wonder how Richard will take the news." Her eyes traveled to the phone. "Will he be happy about this? I hope so. I really need him now." A smile spread across her face. "Maybe we'll get married!" Taking a deep breath, she reached for the phone, but stopped in mid-air. "But then again, he hasn't called lately. Another broken promise." She looked down at the cat sleeping on her lap as she made her decision and dialed Richard's number. "Well, I'll know soon enough."

♋︎

Four weeks earlier, Linda had begrudgingly gotten up earlier than usual to make the hundred-mile drive, on her dime, for the mandatory sales meeting. Yet she looked forward to it because she was excited to see Richard again, even though he hadn't called her since the last meeting.

Once on the road, she enjoyed watching the sunrise and singing along with the radio as she passed thousands of blooming wildflowers along the roadside. The countryside was an artist's dream filled with every color imaginable.

When she reached her destination, she steeled herself for what she was about to face—not so much the business meeting, but the man who presided over it. The man who made her willpower and brain turn to mush.

Linda drove her old car into the upscale hotel's parking lot. *I wonder what Richard's excuse will be this time.* She parked her car and got out. Looking at her reflection in the car's window, she adjusted her inexpensive gray two-piece business suit over her small frame, and then ran her ringless fingers through her pixie-styled brunette hair.

Good enough, she told her reflection then grabbed her large briefcase and began walking toward the hotel. Clickety-clack. Clickety-clack. She looked down at her gray pumps as she walked across the asphalt and began whispering in rhythm to her steps, "I won't, I won't, I won't fall for him again!"

A uniformed man opened the gold and glass door for her. She looked up in his direction, muttered thanks then paused once inside and waited for her eyes to adjust to the dim lighting. A tall woman, who stood a good head over Linda, also dressed in a business suit with a lacy blouse, approached her.

"Hey, you made it!" Elaine greeted her.

Linda had moved to town six months earlier and worked at temporary secretarial jobs. While working at one of the positions, she'd met Elaine who told her about the opportunity to make big money selling insurance and invited Linda to a meeting, similar to the one today. Since that time, they'd grown closer.

Initially, Linda was skeptical about taking a commission-only position on the hope it would bring in quick money. But, after meeting the single and very handsome vice president, who convinced her she could make it in sales, she quickly changed her mind.

Linda looked up at her friend. "Oh, hi Elaine. Yeah, no problem . . . but what a long drive. Why don't they have these meetings in San Antonio rather than Waco?"

"I guess for the convenience of everybody that lives farther up north. Besides, today's meeting should be great. You'll see . . . the drive will be well worth it."

The two women looked around the lobby. It was a flurry of activity as business people from all over the state arrived for the big meeting. Elaine moved closer to Linda and whispered in her ear, "So? How's Richard doing?"

Linda looked at her friend, seeing the secretive smile on her lips. "I wouldn't know any better than you. He hasn't called since the last meeting."

"The bum!"

Linda smiled. "My thoughts exactly." She moved the heavy briefcase from one hand to the other. "Well, let's go in and see if the trip was worth it."

"Okay." The two walked side-by-side into the ballroom where the meeting would soon start.

The huge and elegantly decorated room had plush carpeting, with dark green paisley wallpaper covering the lower half of the walls and mirrors on the upper half, making the room appear even larger.

Although small groups of people were scattered around the room, many of the chairs were already occupied. "What a big crowd today!" Elaine said as both women searched for empty seats. Pointing out two chairs near the back of the room, Elaine said "Over there," then quickly went to claim them with Linda following.

Before slipping her briefcase under her chair, Linda took out a writing pad and pen. Both women scanned the room. A sign reading *R.I.C.H.* covered the podium centered on the platform at the front of the room. Taped to the mirrors behind the platform hung a large banner with the words, *Soar with the Eagles.*

Linda continued to look around and suddenly her heart fluttered irregularly and her stomach tensed when she spotted a very attractive, tall, dark-haired man dressed in an expensive three-piece navy pinstriped suit at the front of the room. Richard. *I still get that feeling every time I even see him!* Then she noticed how he seemed to be happily flirting with several women. *Maybe that's why he hasn't called me?* "What a creep," she said under her breath.

"Linda, don't think anything about that." Linda looked toward Elaine, surprised that she had heard her. Elaine nodded her head toward Richard. "He's probably just talking business."

With hurt in her eyes, Linda lied, "It doesn't matter what he's doing. I don't care."

"What's with you today?" Elaine asked. "You're usually so positive, but something is obviously bugging you. Do you want to talk about it?"

She ignored the concern in Elaine's voice. "Not really." Linda felt Elaine's eyes on her and knew her friend was concerned. She finally glanced at Elaine, but then looked back down. "Well, it's just that I had high hopes for this sales job and after four months I still haven't earned a dime, plus it's costing me money. It's like I'm paying for the privilege of being associated with this company." Linda stopped and looked directly at her friend. "I'm not saying it's your fault, Elaine, I know you wouldn't mislead me." Linda looked around the room at nothing in particular before continuing, "I guess I'm upset with myself. Upset partly because I started in this business believing Richard when he looked at me with those deep dark eyes telling me it was easy, that I'd go far and make more money than I ever dreamed possible, and partly for falling under Richard's spell." Linda's eyes found Richard. "I really thought he cared about me. Live and learn, I guess."

The women who had surrounded him had sat down. Richard picked up the gavel and knocked it a few times on the podium. He flashed his sexy smile while he made eye contact with a few attractive women near the front of the room.

Linda leaned toward Elaine while keeping her eyes on Richard as she whispered, "He doesn't even realize I'm here. He's so blatantly flirting!"

"He's just making them feel welcome—must be new recruits."

Richard's powerful, deep voice came barreling through the speakers placed around the room. "May I have your attention?"

An hour later, Linda still had not written a single note on her pad and stopped listening. *What a waste of time and money this was.* She shook her head. *I'd better face facts and go find a real job tomorrow.*

"Isn't this a great meeting?"

Elaine's whisper brought Linda out of her thoughts. She turned and looked at Elaine in amazement. "Are you kidding? I haven't even taken one note!"

Elaine ignored Linda's negativity.

Richard's voice boomed from all sides of the room. "What do you want to be?" He was doing his usual best to motivate the audience to their feet.

"RICH!" came the desired response.

"What a joke," Linda muttered more to herself than to Elaine. She looked around at the crowd. They were all caught up in his spell.

"Rich!" continued Richard. "R is for responsibility. I is for insuring the world, C is for creative selling, and H is for helping others. It's EASY to be RICH!" The audience cheered and clapped wildly.

The more Linda heard, the more she was disenchanted. *This is a crock! Why did I ever believe in this?* She looked at Elaine whose eyes were glued on Richard. He had totally mesmerized her and the rest of the audience with his charisma . . . again.

"Thanks for coming," Richard smiled at the audience. "I'll see all of you next month!" The crowd rose to its feet, applauding enthusiastically. He thrived on the attention and support of the audience.

Linda bent forward to pull her briefcase out from under her chair. "Well, I'm glad that's over. What a waste of time, money and energy."

"Oh, you're just upset because Richard hasn't called you, Linda. It was a great meeting!"

"Are you kidding, Elaine? It was a rah-rah, get happy session." She held up her notepad for Elaine to see before putting it in her briefcase. "I didn't take a single note or learn a single thing to help me make a sale." Both women stood up and gathered their belongings. "Actually, I don't think I'm going to pursue this 'sales career' anymore. I just can't afford to."

Linda led the way to the room's main corridor where they waited in human traffic to exit. Linda turned to Elaine and rolled her eyes.

"You sure are in the dumps. It just takes some time to learn the ropes."

"And when and where do we learn *the ropes*?" Linda asked. Elaine didn't answer. Something behind Linda held her focus.

"What?" Linda twirled around to face Richard.

"Hi, Linda. I've been meaning to call you." His tone of voice reminded her of a cat purr. "I've been so wrapped up with the business; I guess time just slipped by." He reached out to take her hand. "You forgive me, don't you?"

Linda avoided his hand and turned toward Elaine. "Are you ready to go?"

Not one to easily give up, Richard continued, "I've missed you, Linda. I'm really sorry. Let me make it up to you." He reached out again and took her free hand then gazed deeply into her eyes. "How about dinner, drinks and dancing tonight?"

No, I'm _not_ going to fall for this again! Yet, she felt her resolve starting to flow out of her hand into Richard's warm palm. Linda pulled her hand out of his grasp. "I don't think so, Richard." Linda looked down to avoid his eyes. "We always have a great time together, but then I never hear from you until the next meeting. I'm tired of the game." *Good girl, you told him.*

Richard, obviously determined not to be turned down, reached out for Linda's hand once again. "You're right. I should've called. But I really have missed you." Between those puppy-dog eyes, the velvety smoothness of his deep voice and that knowing smile, her resolve faltered. "I promise you, go out with me tonight, and I'll call every day!"

Linda wanted to believe him. She felt her determination and strength melt away. *Be strong!* she thought. *I can't,* she answered. She felt him squeeze her fingers and looked down at his large warm hand holding hers. "Oh, all right. But, if I don't hear from you again until the next meeting . . . that's it. I mean it, Richard!"

Richard smiled then took a quick look around the room. When his eyes returned to Linda, he said, "It's a deal."

She smiled, yet wondered, *why had he looked around the room? To see if anyone noticed his conquest, or perhaps seeing if there was a better option out there?* She forced her mind to stop wandering. *Stop the insecurities. He wants me!*

Elaine's voice brought her back to the present. "I'll see ya later, Linda. Richard." Then she squeezed behind Linda to make her exit.

Linda turned to smile at her in thanks. "Oh, okay. See ya, Elaine." As she walked away, Richard wrapped his arm around Linda.

Richard had wined and dined Linda, treating her like royalty. Yet, once again, he had not called her since they parted late the following morning.

ᙆᙓ

Linda's palms started sweating as she waited for an answer. *I don't know why I'm so scared to talk to him all of the sudden.* Still no answer. *Maybe, he's not there. I'll just leave a message.* She waited. Suddenly she heard Richard, not the recording, say hello.

"Oh," Linda's voice trembled slightly, "Hi, Richard." He did not respond. "It's Linda."

"Linda?"

I gave him what he wanted and he doesn't even remember me? Anger simmered in the pit of her stomach, yet in a teasing tone she said, "What do you mean 'Linda?' like you don't know!" He did not reply and her anger flowed upward. "How come you haven't called? You promised . . ."

A moment of silence hung in the air before he said, "I've been busy."

His words crushed Linda. But, as usual, she covered her hurt with anger. *Bastard!* her mind screamed, while her calm, controlled voice said, "Oh." She switched the phone to the other ear as she inhaled deeply to gather courage and give Richard the news. "Well, since you're busy, I'll make this quick and to the point. I'm pregnant." She held her breath waiting for Richard's response.

"Who's the father?"

Fed up with his arrogance, she snarled, "JC the second! Who do you think the father is?" Linda's tense

9

words woke up Sweetie. He jumped down to the floor. Linda stood up and walked to the side of the couch as she continued on. With each word her voice climbed a decibel in pitch and volume. "I can't believe you said that! It's yours . . . and what are you going to do about it?" Linda stopped abruptly and took several deep breaths in an attempt to calm herself down.

"Nothing."

"What?"

"Nothing. I don't care about any baby or you. I'm not going *to do* anything about it. It's your problem. Deal with it."

Tears formed in her eyes as the reality of the situation struck Linda. She was angry, hurt and alone. But she'd be damned if she'd let Richard know that. No, for now, she'd focus on her anger. "No, it takes two to tango. It's *our* problem." She took another deep breath then continued, "You know, for being such a hotshot VP of a Fortune 500 company who constantly preaches about responsibility, you sure aren't very responsible." Linda's hands shook, her adrenalin flowed, but she fought to keep control of herself. Very quietly she said, "Thank you, *Dick*. Thanks a lot."

Linda began to gently set the receiver down, but then slammed it. She turned and picked up Sweetie, then held him tightly next to her chest. "Everything will be okay," she said while stretching out on the couch and burying her face in Sweetie's fur.

After a few minutes, Sweetie jumped down and Linda sat up looking at nothing in particular. "Oh Mom, I wish you were here. I've really gotten myself into a predicament this time. I don't know what to do. I don't know anyone well enough in this town to ask for help.

Oh, how I wish you were alive. Who can I turn to, Mom?"

Tears started rolling down Linda's cheeks, dripping onto her lap. A feeling of despair swept over her and slowly she lowered her face into her hands and prayed, *Lord, help me.*

2
OPTIONS

L inda stepped out her front door and looked up at the blue sky. For the past four months, her home had been an efficiency apartment. The complex consisted of several beige brick buildings surrounded by short flowering shrubs, a few tall cottonwood trees, well-manicured lawns and a parking lot that snaked around the buildings. Its appearance contradicted its location in a low-rent, high-crime district of the city. The other tenants kept to themselves and she had yet to meet her closest neighbors. She decided the near-constant sound of sirens kept people inside their apartments—where they felt safe.

Despite her limited budget, she'd done her best to make her studio apartment homey for herself and her beloved cat. Her couch opened out as a bed, and a pair of wooden crates she'd found served as end tables. A folding chair allowed her to sit at a card table that served as both a desk and place to eat. Over the couch, Linda had hung an attractive, yet inexpensive framed print of smoky-blue mountains, and the black-and-white TV, she'd owned since college, sat on the floor in the corner.

Although the carpeting and walls were a drab neutral color, Linda liked the place because of its balcony—the only source of light into the otherwise dark apartment. Linda and her cat spent most of their time on the balcony where they listened to the birds sing in the trees, when the sirens weren't blaring.

Linda touched her still-flat stomach. *Another beautiful day belies the trouble I face.* She looked toward her cat seated on the balcony railing. "I'll be home in a few hours, Sweetie. Love you!" She blew him a kiss, flung her purse over her shoulder then hurried down the stairs to the parking lot.

Her car had no front bumper or grill and dings and dents covered the gray primer-painted body. The interior was not in any better shape. The seats were split, the roof liner drooped and cracks covered the vinyl dashboard. Linda inserted the key into the lock. *Why do I bother locking the car . . . seriously, who would steal it?*

She turned the ignition, but nothing happened. She tried again. Nothing. *Please, not now!* She grabbed a dirty rag from the floor, then got out and popped open the hood and wiggled the battery cables. She closed the hood, wiped off her hands on the dirty rag, then climbed back into the car and tried the ignition again. This time she heard a slow, weak grinding noise, then silence. She rested her forehead on the steering wheel. "Great, just great— dead battery."

Linda climbed out of the broken-down car and looked up at her balcony to see Sweetie still perched on the railing, watching her intently. "Dead again! I guess it's ankle-express time." She looked down at her sandal-clad feet, then back up at her cat. "Or maybe, I can catch the bus. Hope so!" Linda waved goodbye and quickly made her way to the bus stop at the front of the complex.

No bus in sight. Linda looked at her watch. *How will I ever make it in time?* In the distance, Linda heard a loud engine. She looked up and saw a bus coming around the corner. *About time my luck turned around!*

The bus stopped and the doors opened. "How much is the fare to the mall?"

"Fifty cents, Ma'am."

She looked into her purse and pulled out two quarters. "Great, I've got it!" Linda boarded the bus and dropped the coins into the box, then found a window seat near the front.

She didn't talk to a soul on the short trip to the town's mall. After exiting, she stood in the sunshine and waited until the bus drove off before crossing the street to a four-story office building.

In front of the dark brown marble building, a gilded fountain shot water sprays into the air. Linda sat down at the side of the fountain to give herself a moment to gather her courage. She watched small rainbows refracted in the fountain's mist and listened to the peaceful sound of the falling water. *Okay, I'm ready.* She rose and entered the building.

The lobby, a large open area with brown marble walls, a high ceiling and two sets of gold elevator doors on either side of an office directory, was deserted. Off to the side a long hallway led to private offices.

Linda quickly found the suite number she needed, made her way down the empty hallway to her destination, and swiftly entered the door into a small open area. She approached the closed, frosted sliding reception window and rang the bell placed on its windowsill.

A large woman with brown eyes and gray hair opened the window. "Welcome to Faith Services. May I help you?"

"Yes, I had an appointment at two o'clock," said Linda, "I know I'm late, but my car wouldn't start and I ended up taking the bus." She nervously rambled on, "Do I need to reschedule?"

The woman looked down at an appointment book, then back up at her and smiled. "You must be Linda?"

Linda detected kindness in the woman's eyes and wanted to trust her, yet felt like a scared animal posed to take flight from the smallest thing. "Yes, ma'am."

The woman spoke in a slow, deep voice laced with an educated southern drawl. "Well, dear, I'm glad you made it! Sometimes people just change their minds. They don't show at all. And, no, you don't need to reschedule." The woman extended her large, tanned hand through the window, "By the way, I'm Pearl." Linda shook her hand. "As you can see, we're not too busy today." Pearl gestured to the vacant chairs around the waiting room then picked up a clipboard holding some forms and handed it, along with a pen, to Linda. "Here, dear, please have a seat and fill out this questionnaire. Aimee will see you in just a few minutes."

Linda thanked the woman and accepted the clipboard and pen, then sat in the nearest chair. Pearl silently slid the glass window shut.

After she'd completed the paperwork, she looked around the waiting room. Everything in the room was white: the ceiling, floor tiles, walls, chairs and bookstand; except for the huge, bright green Boston fern hanging in a gold planter.

As she admired the healthy plant, the door next to the sliding glass window opened and Pearl stood in the doorway. "Please follow me."

Linda picked up the clipboard and her purse then followed her down a short hall with three closed doors.

Pearl opened the door on the right and stood to the side to allow Linda to enter the room. "Please have a seat, Linda. I'll take your paperwork to Aimee and she'll be with you shortly." She accepted the clipboard from Linda and closed the door as she left the room.

Linda sat down in one of the two chrome and white vinyl chairs that faced the desk in the center of the room and looked around the small office. A dark green armed leather chair sat behind the desk, a brown wooden bookcase stood in one corner and a table with a TV and VCR occupied the opposite corner. The numerous plants scattered around the room gave it a fresh, homey feel. A few posters about unplanned pregnancies hung on the walls and several framed photographs of smiling groups of people holding babies were displayed on the shelves and desk.

The door opened and a woman of medium build with dark blonde hair, worn in a simple ponytail, entered. "Hello, Linda." The woman held out her hand. "I'm Aimee."

"Hi," Linda said quietly as she shook the woman's hand.

Aimee sat down behind the desk, leaned forward and asked, "How are you feeling?"

Linda looked down to avoid Aimee's penetrating green eyes and lied, "Fine."

"Linda, I know you're confused and scared. But your being here today tells me you want to make the best decision possible."

Linda tried desperately to keep a grip on her emotions. She felt liked she was in a maze with no idea of which way to proceed. With no remaining family, she didn't know where to turn or who to trust. Something, though, told her she could trust this woman. She lifted her head and looked into Aimee's eyes. In them, she saw caring.

"You know," Aimee said, "they say the eyes are the windows to our souls. What I see in your eyes is a very scared girl trying to find someone she can trust."

Linda blinked with surprise. "You're right."

"Linda, you can trust me. Anything we discuss here, in this office, will remain here."

Linda nodded in response and Aimee smiled. "How far along are you?"

Linda's eyes returned to her hands that remained clenched in her lap. "Eleven weeks."

"I've got to ask you some rather personal questions, Linda, and I know some of them will be difficult for you to answer, but the more information you can give me, the more I can help you. Are you willing to try?"

Without looking up, Linda nodded. Aimee pushed ahead. "Is the baby's father in the picture? Is he involved in the decision?"

Remembering the words of her final conversation with Richard, she felt her composure slipping. Tears stung the back of her eyelids. "No. He said it's my problem, to do what I wanted. To *deal* with it." Those words still hurt her. First one tear, then another, slipped out from behind her eyelashes. She took in a large gulp of air before saying, "He doesn't care about the baby . . . or me." The words hung in the air. With no anger to hide behind, the reality that Richard wouldn't marry her and that she was all alone, hit home. She mourned for a lost love. She mourned for a lack of a supportive family or friends. Her shoulders slumped and she began to sob having finally admitted the situation to Aimee, and herself.

Linda needed to get the tears and emotions out, in order to move forward. While she cried, slowly releasing her built-up anger and disappointment and fear of the unknown, Aimee stepped around the desk. She moved the other chair closer to her, then sat down and placed her hands gently over Linda's.

"I'm sorry, Linda. I know this can be the toughest of times—when the father abandons you. But, you will survive. You have others who care about and love you, who will see you through this."

Linda shook her head as a new wave of tears overtook her. She couldn't look up. "I don't have anyone!"

Aimee moved closer to wrap her arm around Linda's heaving shoulders to give her comfort. They sat that way in silence, except for Linda's sobbing, for several minutes. Aimee broke the silence. "Linda, you've come to Faith Services, which makes me assume you believe in God or a superior being, am I correct?"

Linda nodded.

"You always have God's love, you know."

Linda nodded again as her tears ebbed and she wiped her eyes dry with the tissue Aimee handed her. "Thank you."

Aimee patted Linda's shoulder. "You're welcome. Now, Linda, I'm sure you have some questions for me. But first, I've still got to ask you some hard questions, ready?" Linda nodded. "Have you made any decisions about what you're going to do about this pregnancy or are you just checking out options at this point?"

Linda maintained eye contact with Aimee as she replied in a steady voice, "I'm checking out the options."

Aimee nodded. "That's fine, Linda." Linda's glance returned to her folded hands on her lap. "Do you want to carry your baby to term?"

Linda jerked her head up at the question and looked directly at Aimee. "Are you asking me if I want an abortion? If you are, there's no way!" She swallowed hard, lowered her eyes, and then continued. "I'm thirty years old. I had planned to be married at twenty, have my first child at twenty-five." She took a deep breath and with a twisted grin said, "I blew that plan, huh?" She straightened up and continued, "The point is, this may be the only baby I ever have. I can't; I just can't have an abortion." Linda looked up to see Aimee's reaction. "Can you understand where I'm coming from?"

Aimee held Linda's hands in her own. "I understand. So, Linda, are you prepared to carry the baby to full-term and raise it as a single mother?"

Linda looked over at the photographs on Aimee's desk of the happy people with the babies. "The truth is, I'd love to. Lord knows I have more than enough love to give this baby." Linda looked back at Aimee, "but the reality is, I'm old enough to know that love is not enough. It takes time, energy and money. I don't make enough to even afford to keep my car running. I don't see how I could afford to raise a child." She stopped to take a breath. "I don't want to live on hand-outs, welfare or that stuff. What kind of life is that to raise a child in? I want this baby. I want to raise this baby, but I need to think of the baby's needs first."

She took another deep, shaky, breath then looked back down. "The baby needs a stable home and I need money to keep it clothed, fed, schooled, and cared for. The baby needs someone there to raise him. I want to be that person, but I know I can't." Linda removed her hands from Aimee's and reached for a tissue as the floodgates reopened. All the thoughts that had floated around in her head these past few weeks rushed out of her mouth. Once she'd started, she couldn't stop. "How can I work full-time to make the necessary money and still be there with my baby? The reality is, I can't."

Finished letting out all her jumbled feelings, Linda looked at Aimee in despair. "What choice do I have? So, in answer to your question, no, I don't think I can raise this baby on my own."

Linda looked at the photographs once again, then back at Aimee, before her eyes returned to her hands tightly holding the tissue in her lap.

Aimee absorbed all that Linda had shared with her. She was pleased she had opened up to her, but now it was her turn to be as honest with Linda about her options as she possibly could be, without swaying her to make her decision one way over another. "I know what a difficult decision you are facing, Linda. It's probably the hardest decision of your life. Have you thought about adoption?" Linda looked at Aimee with a blank expression as she continued, "Do you think you could carry this baby to full-term and then entrust his or her upbringing to a loving couple?"

Linda sat quietly for a few seconds. Her bottom lip began to quiver. She took the last tissue as she shook her head vehemently. The tears started coming again. "I don't know. I just don't know what to do. I know I can't raise the baby by myself, but I can't bear the thought of never seeing my child again. But what other choice is there? Do you see why I'm so screwed up? I need help!" Linda dried her tears then lifted her head and looked Aimee in the eyes. "That's why I'm checking things out. I just don't know what to do."

Aimee squeezed her hand then replaced the empty tissue box on the desk with a fresh one. Linda reached out for another tissue as Aimee returned to the chair next to her. "That's why you came here, Linda, because hopefully, I will show you options that will help you make the best decision. A decision you are happy with."

Linda laughed through her tears. "Talk about *Mission Impossible.*"

Aimee smiled. "At least your sense of humor is still with you—that's good. You'll need it." Aimee stood up and walked over to her file cabinet. She pulled out some pamphlets then returned to Linda. "There are different types of adoptions, Linda. There are closed adoptions, which I believe you were referring to. Closed, meaning the records are sealed. You walk away from your baby with no further contact."

Linda nodded. "I thought that was the only kind of adoption." She reached for yet another tissue and blew her nose before returning her attention to Aimee.

"The other option," Aimee looked directly into Linda's eyes, "is an adoption where you maintain contact with your baby throughout your lifetime. The records remain open. It's referred to as 'open adoption.'"

Aimee placed the pamphlets on the desk in front of Linda. She glanced at the pamphlets, but did not pick them up. "Open?"

"Yes. Although many people still are not aware of them, they are becoming more and more commonplace. Open adoptions are based on openness, honesty and give the adopted child the access to his or her biological parent's medical history without the red tape."

Linda sat up straighter and listened intently to Aimee.

"As a birthmother, it's your responsibility to choose the parents for your child. All of your medical bills are taken care of by the adoption agency, and after the birth of your child, you have the option to stay in touch with the adoptive family and your child. Some birthmothers even visit with the adoptive families year after year!"

A glimmer of hope sparkled in Linda's eyes as she reached for the pamphlet on the desktop. "Hmmm . . . this sounds almost too good to be true. I don't see where anybody loses with this arrangement."

Aimee smiled. "Would you be interested in learning more about this option, Linda?"

She looked at the pamphlet then back to Aimee. "Maybe. Until just now, I'd never heard about open adoption. How long has this type of adoption been going on? Why isn't the public more aware of it?"

"I'll tell you what, Linda," Aimee said, "why don't you join us here tomorrow evening for our monthly birthmother support group meeting. I think all your questions will be answered. We'll show a film that gives the history of open adoption, presents all the facts and procedures for pursuing open adoption for your baby, and hopefully, answers all of your questions. Plus, you'll have the opportunity to meet with birthmothers from all walks of life who have faced what you're facing. Will you come?"

She considered it for a moment. "It can't hurt to look into it."

"Great, the meeting starts at seven. I'll see you then."

Linda stood up, looking directly into Aimee's eyes. "Okay . . . and thanks, Aimee."

3
THE MEETING

The following morning Linda purchased a new car battery. It took her a few hours to remove the dead one then install and correctly attach the new one. This time when she turned the key, the car started right up.

Linda felt mighty proud of herself as she stepped into the shower that afternoon to wash the grease and grim from her body.

As she shut off the water, she looked down and touched her stomach. *If only I could figure out the best way to fix things for this little one.*

CRSO

The day's brightness ebbed into dusk as Linda pulled her old car into the parking lot of the tall office building. The spotlights shining up from the ground towards the structure created a glamorous appearance and the lights in the fountain's base created sparkles in the cascading water. Together, it looked magical.

Linda parked her car and scooted out. *Yeah, I'm going to lock you now. Even though you don't look so good, you're running great!*

She went directly to the office where she had been yesterday. This time the sliding glass window had a sign taped to it that read: *Meeting Straight Back.* She walked through the open door and down to the room at the end of the hall.

The large carpeted room had upholstered chairs and two couches arranged in a semi-circle. Against the far wall stood two tables covered with bowls of chips, nachos, candies, bottles of soda, plastic plates and cups.

Several women, ranging in age from thirteen to forty, and a few men sat on the furniture. Aimee and Pearl stood in the back of the room near the TV and VCR.

As Linda entered, Aimee walked over to her. "I'm glad you made it, Linda. I want you to feel at home here." She turned toward the others in the room while she held Linda's hand. "Everyone, I want you to welcome Linda. She has come here tonight to meet you and learn more about open adoption."

In unison, everyone greeted Linda. *Oh boy, that sounded like an AA meeting . . . I don't know about this.*

Aimee let go of her hand to indicate an empty chair. "Why don't you sit over there, Linda?"

Linda sat down, crossing her arms and legs, and then looked around at the faces.

A few minutes later, Aimee walked to the middle of the room. "Alright, everyone is here. Tonight, I thought we'd share stories first, and then watch a film about other successful open adoptions. Let's begin!" Aimee looked toward a skinny woman, with long, straight blonde hair and big blue eyes dressed in blue jeans, a tee-shirt and tennis shoes. She appeared to be in her mid-twenties. "Connie, will you go first, please?"

Connie sat on a couch next to a man whose hand rested on her knee. She smiled then began to speak. "I found myself with an unplanned pregnancy nearly eight years ago. I felt lost, cheap, an outcast and scared to death." She smiled at Pearl. "Then I met Pearl. Pearl helped me to see the light at the end of the longest, darkest tunnel of my life. With her help, I located the perfect adoptive parents for my unborn child. And now, nearly eight years later . . . we are all still one big happy family!" Connie beamed. "We've spent every Christmas and all of my son's birthdays together since the day he was born."

Connie paused as she looked around the room. "If anyone had told me this was possible and that I would be a part of my son's life for the rest of my life, I wouldn't have believed them. Even at the point in the hospital when I signed the adoption papers, a big part of me still didn't believe the 'open' part would work. I braced myself for the fact that once my son left the hospital, I would probably never see him again." Connie glanced at each of the mothers-to-be before going on. "Well, guess what? Not only did it work, but it went beyond my wildest expectations. I am now a part of my son's life and a much-loved member of his adoptive family! So, yes, ladies, it *does* work. Have faith and trust that your situation will be just as rewarding as mine turned out to be."

Connie looked at the man seated next to her, then looked back at the women in the room. "Oh, one last thing. No, your life does not stop when you give birth. I thought I would never date again after finding myself alone and pregnant. But time does heal." Connie clasped the man's hand that rested on her knee and smiled at him.

"Four years after giving birth, I met this terrific guy and we've now been married two years AND we just learned we're expecting our first child in about eight months!" Connie's face glowed with happiness as she ended her speech.

Everyone in the room applauded and congratulated her.

Linda had sat silently through the story. By the end of the meeting, a calmness filled her body and she had, without noticing, uncrossed her arms and legs.

4
SEARCHING

Four months quickly passed. Linda was now seven months into her pregnancy and it showed. She sat in a chair facing the desk with several three-ring binders scattered haphazardly around her feet. She began going through yet another three-ring binder balanced on her knees while Aimee, with her back to Linda, worked on her computer.

"Oh, Aimee, I'm just not finding anybody who sticks out as 'the ones.'" She turned another page in the binder. "Why did I have to wait so long to start going through the couples wanting to adopt? I'm scared I'm not going to find the 'perfect couple.'"

Aimee turned around to face Linda. "Don't despair, Linda."

"But we're getting down to the wire here. What if I can't find anybody?"

Aimee smiled. "You'll find the perfect couple. Keep your faith!"

Linda turned the page, reading yet *another* letter from yet *another* couple that wanted to adopt a child. She shook her head and moved to the next page. "I wish I had your confidence! How can you always be so upbeat, Aimee?"

Aimee reached over and squeezed her hand. "It's part of the job description. Plus, I've seen too many wonderful people come together. I know you'll find who you're looking for!"

Linda returned Aimee's smile then returned to the binder and continued reading as Aimee returned to her computer work.

As she finished looking at the last of the binders with no success, she slowly slid down to the floor to gather up the other binders. Aimee came over to help her. "All done?"

"Yeah, but with no luck." Together they put all the binders back on the bookshelf in the corner.

As she helped Linda back up to the chair, Aimee asked, "Nobody, eh?"

"Nope." Linda opened her purse and looked for her car keys. "I'm beginning to think that maybe someway . . . somehow, I should just try to raise this baby on my own."

"That's your choice, Linda. But just think long and hard about it. Don't let yourself be forced into a situation that shouldn't be. Besides, God works in mysterious ways. If it's meant to be, the right couple will come along for you. You'll see."

Linda nodded as she found her keys. "I'll keep that in mind. But I don't have much time left. I'll just have to pray harder, I guess." She slowly got up from her chair and slung her purse over her shoulder then Aimee escorted her to the closed office door. As Aimee reached for the handle, a soft knock sounded and Pearl popped her head in.

Aimee pulled the door fully open. "Hi, Pearl. Come on in."

She entered the room and greeted Aimee and Linda with a smile. "This just came in and I thought you *and* Linda might want to take a look at it." Pearl held out a manila envelope toward Aimee.

Aimee reached for the envelope and thanked her. After Pearl left, Aimee peeked into the envelope then handed it to Linda. "Maybe the answer to your prayers just arrived."

5
THE LETTER

Time continued to slip by. In just two short weeks, the baby within her would be born and go to its new family. But first, Linda had something very special she wanted to create for her child.

Seven weeks earlier, Linda had selected, what she believed to be, the ideal couple to adopt her baby. She discovered them in the envelope Pearl delivered. The couple was around the same age as Linda, from the same state, of the same religion and of the same educational background. Plus, like Linda, they suffered from allergies. She felt confident this couple would know how to take care of the baby, should it inherit the lung problems. Her final gift was to write a letter to her unborn child telling it why she gave it up for adoption.

Linda had waited to begin this final step until the right words came to her. It would be hard, but she couldn't postpone writing it any longer. Today was already a hard day: Thanksgiving and the fifteenth anniversary of her mother's death. She hated Thanksgiving and, even more, hated being alone on this day. Yet, here she sat alone, except for Sweetie—stretched across the table. "I guess this is the perfect time to get started." She looked at Sweetie as though he understood her completely. Linda patted her huge tummy. "Knowing what sex he is makes writing this letter easier. I wonder if he'll be on time?" Linda looked down and smiled at her stomach.

The cat looked at her. Lately, he had not been acting normal. It seemed he was jealous of her pregnancy and tended to hiss at her constantly. She stroked the cat's back and said, "Soon this chapter of our lives will be over, Sweetie, and things will be back to normal for you."

She got up and walked into the kitchen to prepare her Thanksgiving dinner—a bologna sandwich with a glass of milk. She placed her meal on the folding table then grabbed the box of teddy bear stationery she had purchased the day before to use for this very special letter. Linda slowly sat down at the table and took a bite of her Thanksgiving dinner as she thought about how to start the letter to this little person within her.

She placed the sandwich back on the paper plate and then picked up the pen as the words began to flow:

> *My dearest Christian,*
>
> *It is Thanksgiving, two weeks before you are due to enter this world. I wonder what it is like for you in my tummy with warmness surrounding you? Can you feel my moods? My happiness? Hear me singing? I think you can. You kick when I sing. Come on, I'm not that bad!* ☺

Linda stood up to stretch. Being so large was a bit awkward and she couldn't stay in one position for very long. She placed her hands at the small of her back and stretched backwards and then returned to her chair. She reached forward to pet her cat for a moment then picked up the pen and continued to write.

> *I write this letter knowing that someday either you or your parents will read this to you. I want to tell you so much. Where do I start? I guess the best place is at the beginning.*
>
> *I discovered I was pregnant four weeks after you were conceived. At first I was really surprised, but happy. But when I realized your biological father wouldn't marry me, I had to do some serious soul searching . . .*

Linda stopped writing for a moment, took a drink of the milk, petted her cat's back then continued writing to her unborn child.

> *As a single mom, I couldn't afford to give you the lifestyle, education or a two-parent home—which I feel is so important and which you deserve. So I made the only choice I thought was right: open adoption.*
>
> *You're so important to me. Whether I see you or not, I want you to grow up being loved and happy.*

The pages went blurry as unshed tears filled Linda's eyes. She stopped writing for a moment to dab them away with a tissue. *It's just my highly emotional state,* she told herself before returning to the letter.

> *Having you within me these last several months has been a joy that God blessed me with. I don't*

even mind that I've gained nearly fifty pounds. I just want you to be healthy.

I don't know what your parents will name you, but I named you Christian: a good, strong name. I think it will fit you.

Although your adoptive parents, who take you into their home and hearts are truly your parents, I will always hold a special place for you in my heart.

Linda put the pen down as she took a deep, shaky breath. Her cat stood up on the table and stretched then rubbed his body against her face. "Just a minute, Sweetie, let me finish this."

The cat jumped off the table and she continued the letter.

Well, my precious cat, who is also my best friend, wants some loving. So I'll end this letter. In closing, remember that life is a gift from God. Cherish it as you would your most prized possession. Know that people love and care deeply for you and most importantly that God loves you, watches over you and takes care of you. Please believe in your dreams and they will come true.

Tears trickled out from the corners of Linda's eyes and rolled down her cheeks. She wiped them away, trying not to lose her train of thought.

Shoot for the stars, my son.
God bless you.
Your Birthmother

Linda put the pen down and took several deep breaths to steady her emotions, before she wiped away her tears. "Wow. That was tough. I'm glad it's done." She picked up her cat, kissed him on top of his head and then set him on the floor. "Time to eat." She picked up the sandwich, tore off some of the bologna and held it out to her cat. "Happy Thanksgiving, Sweetie."

6
THE MORNING

That Sunday morning the sun had just peeked over the horizon when Sweetie rubbed his face into Linda's. She reached over, with eyes closed, to cradle Sweetie next to her. "You want to go out, eh?"

The cat replied with a low meow.

"Oh, all right. Give me a minute." Linda stretched her legs and arms. The sunlight streaming through the sliding glass door greeted her as she opened her eyes.

Linda had gotten so big with child that she no longer could sleep in her hide-a-bed. A few weeks earlier, she had gotten stuck between the bars and it had taken her over forty-five minutes to get free. Since she didn't have anybody to help her, she decided it was safer not to pull out the hidden bed, but rather just sleep on it as a couch.

As she slowly rolled herself off, the cat jumped down and waited patiently for her at the front door. She waddled over and squatted down to pet Sweetie then opened up the door so he could go outside. "Be good, have fun and don't go far!" The cat scooted outside. "I love you. I'll check on you in an hour."

She didn't think twice about letting Sweetie out for an hour each morning. He had his tags and always stayed in sight. He particularly liked to nap curled up under the bottom of the stairs or sprawled out on the hood of Linda's car.

She waddled back to the couch, lay down on her side and quickly fell back to sleep.

Her dreams suddenly filled with screams. Sweetie's screams. Linda's eyes flew open. She heard another scream. It wasn't a dream. She pushed herself up as fast as she could. "Sweetie!" Linda yelled. "I'm coming!"

She wore only a large tee-shirt and panties. For a split second she thought about throwing on a robe and grabbing a broom, but when she heard her cat scream again, instinct took over and she ran to the door, knowing something was terribly wrong.

She opened the door to her apartment and looked down the stairs that descended to the parking lot filled with shabby vehicles. She heard another scream to her right. She looked to the small grassy area located at the corner of her apartment building and saw Sweetie trapped by two dogs. The large, powerful Japanese Akita, weighing over a hundred pounds, had pinned the cat upside-down on the ground with its mouth. The smaller pit bull held one of the cat's back legs in its mouth. There was no blood. The cat looked up at Linda with fear in his eyes.

Linda yelled over to the dogs, her volume increasing with each word. "Hey, what do you think you're doing? *Let him go!*"

Neither dog released their hold. She glanced around for help, but no one was in sight. Without thinking or realizing any potential danger, she started down the stairs toward the dogs as fast as she could.

As she reached the bottom landing, the dogs looked up and released their hold on the cat. Her cat righted himself and scrambled to safety under a nearby car. Linda quickly moved to the dogs and grabbed the collar of the pit bull. He immediately sat down at her side. The larger dog, however, darted to the car, sniffing and growling. Saliva dripped off his exposed teeth.

With the pit bull sitting contentedly by her side as she held his collar, Linda tried to talk some sense into the Akita. In a soft, calm voice she said, "Stop that. Leave him alone."

The Akita stopped growling and swung his head toward Linda. He looked her squarely in the eyes and when she returned his stare, the dog suddenly lunged at her. He dug his teeth into her right arm while swinging his head violently from side to side as he tried to rip it off.

With more surprise than pain, Linda shouted, "Ow!" She had not expected the dog to sink its teeth into her and she kept calm until pain set in. Then she knew she had to fight back to protect herself and the baby. She needed her other arm, so released the pit bull's collar. At that same moment, Sweetie dashed out from the safety of the car to run up a cottonwood tree. "Run, Sweetie, run!" She watched in horror as the pit bull caught him before he reached safety.

The Akita continued tearing at her arm, which by now, was going numb. She blocked her belly with her left arm while the dog continued to jerk her right arm back and forth. Her blood flowed onto the dog and ground. She looked up to the sky and screamed in pain, *"HELP! Somebody HELP ME!"*

Just as suddenly as the dog had attacked, he released her arm. Linda began to run, but from the corner of her eye, she saw the dog leap at her. In a protective reflex, she cringed up her shoulders just as the dog's powerful jaws wrapped around the back of her head and neck, narrowly missing her jugular vein.

The dog lifted Linda off the ground and whipped her body back and forth, like a rag doll. Keeping her left arm around her stomach to protect the baby, she used the elbow of her injured arm to blindly jab the head of the dog behind her, over and over and over again; all the while hysterically crying at the top of her lungs, *"**HELP! MY GOD, SOMEBODY HELP ME!**"* Her strength drained and her blood sprayed everywhere with each blow to the dog's forehead. Still nobody came to her rescue.

Why won't anyone help? I can't keep this up! Oh God, give me the strength to get through this. With the force of desperation, she smashed the dog between the eyes with her elbow one last time. The dog yelped in pain and released Linda. She fell abruptly to her knees on the rough asphalt and the dog ran off.

Skin and muscle hung from the bone of her arm. With each beat of her heart, blood spurted out of her neck and flowed from the teeth marks in her arm and cuts on her legs.

Linda struggled to lift her head, but she was too weak. *My baby. My cat.* She prayed *help them, help me, Lord,* before her eyes closed and she collapsed to the ground.

7

HELP

Several minutes passed before Linda's eyes fluttered open. Despite the bright sunshine, an eerie quietness prevailed. Not even a bird chirped. She looked at the blood-covered asphalt—her blood. She slowly pushed herself up with the good arm and with the other arm, now throbbing with pain, covered her stomach. She looked closely at her forearm. The skin was ripped away, exposing the muscle, and blood seeped out. She felt something slowly moving down her neck. Thinking it was a gnat, she swiped at it and touched something warm and slimy. She looked at her fingertips. Deep-red blood covered them. *Oh my God! I've got to get help.*

The nearest apartment belonged to her downstairs neighbor. *I need to make it to that door.*

With all the energy she could muster, she slowly stood up. As a wave of dizziness overtook her, she braced herself against the nearest car until it passed. Then she looked again at the neighbor's door. *Please God, give me the strength to reach it.*

Bent over, she slowly inched forward. Although in severe pain, she smiled when she knocked, happy to have reached the door.

Blood covered her shirt, her arm and her legs. She turned and saw a trail of blood from the parking lot to where she stood. Looking down, she noticed the puddle of blood forming at her feet.

Suddenly she felt an excruciating sharp, jabbing pull inside her belly and quickly sucked in air. Her face twisted in pain. She wrapped her arm tighter around her belly. "Oh, please baby, not yet! Not yet!" Leaning her head against the door, she held her breath.

After the pain eased, she heard low music through the door and began slapping it repeatedly with her open palm.

Finally, a young man cracked open the door. He seemed to be around twenty-five years old wearing only boxer shorts and appeared as if he had just woken up. The young man left the door chain secured while he stared at Linda.

Annoyance showed on his face when he noticed the bloody palm prints Linda had left on his door. "It's the crack of dawn. What do you want?"

Breathlessly she answered, "Help . . . me. Call 9-1-1. Dogs . . . attacked . . . me."

The man looked her over slowly, head to toe, and then returned his glare to the blood on his door. "I don't want to get involved," he said coldly, and with that, closed the door in her face.

Dumbfounded, Linda leaned back against the closed door, slowly shaking her head. *How can a person turn away from someone so obviously in need of help?* Tears welled up as she realized nobody would help her. A feeling of utter disbelief, devastation and defeat overtook her.

Another sharp stomach pain shattered her thoughts. "EWW!" She slowly blew out air between clenched teeth until the pain eased. She tightened her hold on her stomach as if to keep the baby from coming and closed her eyes. *Hang on baby. Please, hang on! I've got to make it for the sake of you.* She slowly turned around and looked up the stairs to her apartment. *I can do this!* She grabbed a hold of the railing with her good arm and slowly ascended the stairs, stopping every few steps to breathe and gather energy.

Although exhausted, through sheer determination Linda had reached her open door. *Made it!* Now she thought about her next task. *All I have to do is get the phone and bring it out here. Last thing I need is a carpet cleaning bill for bloodstains.*

Hunched over, she staggered to the phone she kept on top of the wooden crate. She grabbed it, stepped back outside, dialed 9-1-1, then leaned against the doorframe for support.

After two rings a female voice answered, "9-1-1. What's your emergency?"

With shallow breaths Linda said, "Help! I've been . . . attacked . . . by . . . dogs. I'm bleeding . . . all over. My arm hurts and . . . I . . . think . . . my baby . . . is coming." Another contraction overtook her. She swallowed hard before answering the operator's next question. "Yes . . . I'm pregnant." *Jeez that's a dumb question.* "I'm due . . . in two . . . weeks."

As the operator asked for her address, Linda looked up and saw the two dogs with her cat swaying between their mouths. "Trace . . . the call . . ." she said before dropping the phone.

With strength she didn't know she possessed, Linda yelled, "Sweetie, I love you!"

At the sound of her voice, the cat lifted its head and looked directly at her. Then, his head dropped as the final breath flowed out of his body.

"N-O-O-O-O-O-O-O!" Linda screamed. "No!" she whispered as an ambulance and squad car raced around the corner. Two officers jumped out of the car. The dogs dropped the dead cat and charged them as Linda slid down the doorframe and crumbled into a limp heap at the top of the stairway.

8
INTERVIEW

Five hours later Linda sat propped up in the bed by numerous pillows in the flower-filled hospital room. Bandages surrounded her head and neck, two IV needles had been inserted into her hand and a spongy Swiss-cheese-looking cast engulfed her right arm.

At the foot of the bed, a chubby man wearing blue jeans balanced a large camera on his shoulder. Its bright light focused directly on Linda. Next to him, a well-dressed, tall, blonde female held a microphone. An older man wearing an Associated Press badge on his lapel stood behind her and next to him, a young woman held a notepad and pen.

The attractive news reporter turned toward the camera. "We are coming to you live from Good Samaritan Hospital with our *Top Story of the Day.*" The woman walked around the side of Linda's bed. "Early this morning two dogs brutally attacked a pregnant woman." The reporter reached out to touch Linda's shoulder in encouragement. "The dogs nearly killed the woman and her baby and, unfortunately, killed her pet cat, Sweetie." Compassion flowed from the reporter's eyes to Linda's.

"I'm happy to report the mother gave birth to a healthy boy who is in the nursery resting comfortably." She returned her eyes to the camera lens. "With me here is Linda Allen, who survived this horrific ordeal."

"Did you have any idea what kind of jeopardy you were placing yourself and your baby into when you encountered those dogs this morning?"

The cameraman zoomed the camera in on Linda as she replied in a steady voice, "No, none. I love animals and had absolutely no fear. I'd never been attacked before, so the thought never crossed my mind."

The cameraman pulled back to include both the reporter and Linda in the shot. "I understand you asked a neighbor to help you. What happened?"

Linda nodded. "I begged him for help and he said, and I quote, *I don't want to get involved,* unquote."

The camera's focus returned to the reporter as she shook her head. "Linda, do you know who owns the dogs?"

"No, I'd never seen them before."

"Why do you think those dogs attacked you, almost killing you and your child?"

Linda sat silent for a moment, fighting back tears. She swallowed the lump in her throat, before she said, "I believe animals give people the purest form of unconditional love. But when they are kept caged up, on chains or are abused, they become vicious. That's all they've learned. I think that's what happened with these two dogs."

"That could be right." The reporter glanced down at the cards in her hands, then back at Linda. "You may or may not know this, but the dogs also charged the police. The police shot and killed both of them. Do you think that was the right thing to do?"

The last thing Linda remembered was Sweetie dying in the dogs' mouths. With that image in her mind, the tears swelled up again. She bit her trembling bottom lip, *there's no way I'm losing it on TV*. After regaining her composure, she looked into the camera. "No, I didn't know that. And, no, I'm not glad. I feel sorry for the dogs because they weren't loved as God had intended them to be. But I don't feel sorry for the dog owner. He didn't and doesn't deserve to have animals if he can't manage them and keep them home."

Linda fought as hard as she could not to cry. "I'm sorry, but I'm really tired," she said softly before closing her eyes to hide the tears.

The news reporter quickly wrapped up the story and the media crew left.

9
NUMB

The sun had set on the worse day of Linda's life. The only light in the room seeped in from under the door to the hospital's hallway. Linda reclined in bed with her eyes focused on the ceiling. She had no thoughts, no feelings, no nothing. Numbness prevailed.

A gentle knock sounded at the door before a man wearing scrubs quietly entered and stopped at Linda's bedside and, using a pen flashlight, checked Linda's IV's, her arm and head bandage. She lay still and continued to stare blankly at the ceiling.

When he'd completed his tasks, he looked at Linda's face. "Oh, you're awake! I don't suppose you remember me. I'm Dr. Jones, the one who put you back together again."

Linda looked at him with eyes devoid of any emotion.

The doctor patted her hand and looked at her with concern. "How are you feeling? Any pain?"

A deep sigh escaped from her lips before she answered. "No, no pain. Only numb. Everything's numb. My heart, my soul, my life."

The doctor was aware of all that had occurred that day and that she had no family to support her. "I know you've been through an awful lot these past twelve hours," he said in an effort to reach out to her. "But, there *is* a light at the end of the tunnel."

The doctor glanced around the room filled with flowers. "Are you still planning on going through with the adoption? I know it's none of my business, but it's not too late to change your mind."

Linda's body stiffened. She looked long and hard at the doctor before shifting her gaze to the night sky outside the room's only window. "No, I won't change my mind. I made a promise and I'm still going through with it." She turned back toward the doctor, "I still can't give him the one thing he needs, a dad."

The doctor's eyes were filled with kindness and understanding as he patted her shoulder. "I understand, Linda."

The doctor started to leave then stopped and turned around. "Well, if you begin to have any pain, just ring the nurses and they'll give you something for it." He took another step then turned halfway. "Try to get some rest tonight. I'll see you tomorrow. Good night."

Once again, Linda was alone.

10

A NEW ENDING

After the doctor left, Linda resumed her diligent watch of the ceiling. "Good night?" she said aloud. "What's good about it?"

She had only seen her son briefly after the emergency C-section and wondered if he felt as terribly alone, unwanted and unloved in the nursery as she felt laying in this bed. She hugged herself, as best as she could, for comfort. Suddenly she desperately wanted to hold Christian and reached for the call button. *I wonder if they'll allow it?*

"Is there any chance I could see my baby?"

"Sure, we'll bring him to you."

A few minutes later a nurse entered the room cradling Christian and carefully put him in Linda's arms. His dark blue eyes were open as she gazed down at him. She soaked in his face, trying to imprint every one of his features in her mind.

"He just ate, so he'll probably fall asleep soon." The nurse said as she stood at the bedside. "I know it's hard for you to hold him with your arm in that cast, so if you'd like, I can put him in a bassinet next to your bed, so he can stay with you for a short while. Would you like that?"

Linda looked up at her with gratitude in her eyes and nodded.

After the nurse had left to give them privacy, Linda slowly rolled onto her side. A feeling of peacefulness filled her soul as she gazed upon the angelic baby sleeping peacefully in the bassinet. After a few moments of drinking in his presence, she reached out intending to stroke the fuzzy black hair covering his head, but stopped before she touched him. Instead, she sat up, turned on the reading light, pulled over the rolling table by her bedside, opened her purse and pulled out the letter she had written to the baby on Thanksgiving Day. *Was that only a few days ago?* She shook her head and then reread the letter. Once done, she realized that she needed to add a bit more to the ending. After fishing a pen out of her purse, she wrote:

> *It is now the night of your birth. You're in the world alive and kicking. Actually, you're quite lucky to be here, but more about that later. You're so sweet and cute and good-natured. You sleep most of the time. You look a lot like me when I was a baby. And, you came into this world a star. Your entrance was covered on TV and in the newspapers.*

She stopped writing for a moment and looked around the room.

> *People who don't even know us have sent flowers.*

49

She could no longer stand the sting of unshed tears and finally let her control go. The tears flowed endlessly, landing on the spongy cast and the teddy bear stationery as she continued writing.

You see, this morning dogs attacked me. Those dogs killed my cat and during it all, my water broke.

Linda relived the entire day as she wrote the events out for her son. She could not stop the endless stream of tears and now her nose dripped as well. She reached for a tissue as she gulped in a few breaths. She cried for all that she had lost and for all that she was about to lose. Sobs racked her body from her very core.

I passed out and the doctors gave me an emergency C-section to deliver you. Then they worked for hours to put me back together again. Kind of like Humpty-Dumpty. Anyway, thank God, you're okay. You're perfect!

In closing, Christian, since you came into the world a star, change the ending of this letter from "Shoot for the stars, my son" to "Go for the galaxy, guy!"

Linda put down her pen. She tried to wipe the tears off her face, but they kept on coming. She rested against the pillow for a few minutes, staring at the ceiling, then she reached over to her son and, placing her hand on his tiny forehead as he slept peacefully, she whispered, "Go for the galaxy, little guy."

11
THE BRINK

By seven the next morning, Linda had decided she really didn't care to live anymore. *What's the point? Once the baby goes to his new family there really is none.* She began crying uncontrollably. She was exhausted from a sleepless night. Each time she tried sleeping, the day's events started replaying in her mind. She pulled yet another tissue out of the box adding to the wad she held to her eyes.

The door opened soundlessly. Aimee discreetly walked in and approached the end of Linda's bed and asked quietly, "Is everything alright?"

Linda swiped at her tears. "Oh, hi Aimee." Although Aimee had become her friend over the last several months, she was still from the adoption agency. Suddenly panic filled Linda's heart. On the verge of hysteria, Linda reached out and grabbed Aimee's hand, "Have you come to take my son away already? I thought I had a few days with him." She didn't want to hear Aimee's answer, and bracing herself for the inevitable, she lashed out, "That's just great. Hit me when I'm down, why don't ya?" Linda rolled over to hide the tears that flowed down her cheeks.

Aimee had been through this so many times before. It never got easier witnessing a birthmother giving away her child to people she'd never met. She knew what a hard time Linda would soon face. She immediately sat in the chair at the side of the bed and held Linda's hand.

She needed to reassure Linda that it was not time . . . yet. Patting her hand, she confirmed that Linda would be able to stay with the baby until she was released from the hospital. "Now, calm down Linda. I came to see how *you* are doing."

Linda withdrew her hand from Aimee's and wiped away her tears as anger took over sorrow's place. "How am I doing?" She met Aimee's eyes. "Just peachy. I mean I've only been attacked by dogs, my cat is dead and my first born will soon be adopted by his new family . . . leaving me totally alone in the world." A sob escaped her lips. "Why wouldn't everything be *alright*?"

Aimee smiled at Linda. "Well, at least you still have that sense of humor. Seriously, Linda, I understand your anger. You are hurt and grieving. Who wouldn't be in your position?" She continued searching Linda's eyes to see if her words had reached her. "You feel like lashing out at anyone that comes near you, don't you?"

Linda nodded.

"I'm here to help you. Just tell me what you need, what you want."

Linda looked at Aimee for a long minute before her eyes traveled to the window to peer out at the world. "It's so sunny out this morning," she said. "It's as if nothing is wrong. My whole world is destroyed, but the rest of the world is happy." Her eyes returned to Aimee. "What I really want, Aimee, is to die." She turned her head into the pillow and squeezed her eyes shut to fight the tears that threatened to once again overflow. "God, just let me die," she whispered.

Aimee stood up and leaned over Linda. She hugged her for a moment. The room was filled with a heavy silence. Softly, she said, "Linda, you don't mean that . . ."

Linda nodded her head with vengeance, but kept her eyes tightly closed. "Oh, yes I do! What's the point of living? Everything I love or loved is going or gone."

Aimee realized Linda was serious. She looked up, as if to ask God for his help to reach out and pull Linda out of the darkness, praying that God give her the right words to help Linda. She sat back down in the chair.

"God loves you and he's not going to leave you," she said softly.

Linda opened her eyes. An almost hysterical laughter bubbled up within her. "God loves me? What a joke! Why did He make it so that I just gave birth to a son I can't keep? Why did He let Sweetie die?" She took a deep breath and then continued on. "Yeah, right. God loves me. Tell me more."

Aimee reached out to hold Linda's hand. "He does! And he's going to see you through this."

Linda withdrew her hand and turned to look at Aimee. "He's going to show me that if this doesn't kill me, it'll make me stronger? Is that it, Aimee? I'd settle for the killing." she said then looked away. "Thanks, anyways."

Aimee stood up and walked around the bed. She noticed the letter addressed to Christian on the table and picked it up.

"Linda, is this the letter you wrote to your son?"

"Yeah."

"Do you mind if I read it?"

"Knock yourself out."

Linda watched Aimee pick up the letter and saw tears fill her eyes as she read it. When Aimee finished, she placed it back on the table then turned toward Linda. "Linda, how can you tell your son that life is a precious gift to be treasured, when you're telling me you want to throw yours away?"

Linda mumbled, "Things change."

"Yes, they do," said Aimee. "But with every door that closes, a window opens."

Linda listened, but closed her eyes.

"It may seem that yesterday was the darkest dawn of your life, but I know and believe that God has opened another window for you." Aimee continued, "A window, somewhere to let in the morning light of new beginnings that God has planned for you. You may not see that window right now, but it's there. You just need the courage and willpower to find it. Don't give up, Linda! There's too much ahead for you." Aimee smiled as she put her hand over Linda's. "And that precious little boy you brought into the world is loved by God as well as by you. He will grow into a wonderful loving man." Aimee squeezed Linda's hand. "Do you really want to miss all that by asking God to let you die?"

Linda turned her head away in shame. Neither of them moved. After a few minutes of silence, Linda slowly focused on Aimee's hand resting over her own and, as if it were a lifeline, she grabbed it. She looked up into her eyes and said, "Thanks for being here, Aimee."

Aimee squeezed her hand and smiled.

12
GOODBYE

Linda had spent the last four days getting to know her son, holding him, gazing into his blue-black eyes, playing with his tiny fingers and toes and marveling at his perfection. She had enjoyed the time immensely. The love she felt for this little person was indescribable. Yet, she knew in her heart she could not give him the life he deserved and knew that adoption was the best choice. She prayed the adoption would be truly "open" so that she could visit with him throughout the years.

Lately, Linda had heard horror stories from other birth moms—stories about how the birthmothers had given their children to the adoptive families, only to never hear from or see them again. She prayed this would not be the case for her and her son. She truly believed and felt in her heart that the adoptive parents she had chosen were honest, trustworthy and honorable. She trusted she would see her son again.

For now, she sat in bed holding him, looking down on his precious sleeping face. The doctor had signed her release papers and that meant the day had arrived for her son to go to his new home.

Aimee walked in with another woman. "Hi Linda, this is Norma, the adoptive parent's caseworker."

"Nice to meet you, Norma." Linda steeled herself. The time to say goodbye to her little boy had come.

Setting a pen and a clipboard with several papers attached to it on the bed, Aimee said, "I've got some forms for you to sign, Linda."

Linda looked from one woman to the other. "Can I continue holding my baby while I sign?"

"I don't see any problem with that," Aimee said.

Linda began signing the forms. Between each signature, she looked down at her sleeping son in her arms and told him it was for the best. It was because she loved him so very much that she had to do this. Secure with the knowledge that she was doing the right thing, she did not shed a single tear. After signing the forms, she handed them back to Aimee.

"After these are processed," Aimee explained, "you will be mailed a copy." Linda nodded.

Aimee and Norma stood for a few moments watching Linda cradle her son for the last time.

Finally Aimee spoke up, "It's time, Linda."

Linda nodded not taking her eyes off her son. "I know. I guess I'm ready." She lifted her son and looked him over intently, trying to memorize everything about him. Then she cradled his little face against her cheek and whispered in his ear, "I love you so much. Please grow into a fine strong man and please, oh please, let me be a part of your life . . . even if it is just a little piece. I love you."

After a few moments, she handed the child to Norma, who said her goodbyes and then left the room. Linda's son was gone.

Linda pulled her knees up to her chin and wrapped her arms around her legs. She began rocking as powerful sobs wracked her body. Aimee, moved to tears, sat on the bed and embraced her.

13
BURIAL

Linda looked out the window at the overcast sky. *By now, he's probably in the arms of his new parents.*

It was time for Linda to go home, but she didn't have anything to wear since her nightshirt was torn and covered with dried blood. Nor did she have a ride home. *Maybe Elaine would help me.* Linda reached for the phone.

Thirty minutes later Elaine walked into the room carrying a small bag. She had brought Linda a large button down shirt to wear and some stretch pants. It took both of them to get the shirt over Linda's bandages. After Linda got the stretch pants on, she sat on the bed and looked at Elaine.

"It feels so weird, Elaine."

"What does?"

"Everything. Just everything. It's almost as if the last several days were a really bad nightmare. Like I never was pregnant, or had a child, or those dogs never attacked me, and Sweetie isn't dead. I feel as if I'll go home and open the door and Sweetie will be there to greet me, just like he always does."

Elaine put her arm around Linda and looked at her. She understood that denial was her friend's defense to deal with all that had happened. If she didn't remember it, it wouldn't hurt. Yet, Elaine knew the reality of it would hit full force the minute Linda entered her apartment.

"Linda, I wish it wasn't true, that your baby was here for you, that Sweetie was home waiting for you, but the reality is, that's not the way it is." Elaine hugged her friend before packing the rest of her meager belongings into the small bag.

Linda slowly stood up and made her way to the door of the hospital room.

"I'll take you home and stay there as long as you need me," Elaine said as she joined her. "You ready?"

Linda took one final look around the room. "Yeah." The two women walked out arm-in-arm.

CRSO

Elaine opened the apartment door and let Linda pass. Linda stopped in front of the couch as she looked around. "Funny, it's as if nothing changed . . . but everything has. Sweetie isn't running up to greet me . . ." She wrapped her arms around herself.

Elaine noticed the color drain out of Linda's face. "Maybe we should go out to eat."

"No, I'm not hungry." Linda looked around again, then at Elaine. While in the hospital, she had asked Elaine to do her a favor. "Did you bury Sweetie where I asked you to?"

"Yes. He's in the bluebonnet field."

Linda closed her eyes and nodded. "I need to see it, to convince myself that he really is dead. I need to do this for closure. Would you take me there?"

Elaine agreed and the two women exited the dark and lonely apartment.

A slight breeze blew that November afternoon as Elaine stopped the car at the edge of the field. She got out and walked around to help her friend. Linda still had all the stitches in her right arm and head and had to wear the funny-looking cast.

Elaine guided Linda up to the freshly-dug grave. A brief early morning rain shower had left the soil a little muddy. Linda squatted down then placed her hand over the moist soil. "Oh Sweetie," she whispered, "I'm so sorry I couldn't save you." Linda gulped in a breath of cool air as the tears began again. "I tried, Sweetie, I tried." Linda looked up to the sky. "How am I going to live without my best friend?" she said, then sank down on her knees to the earth. Her shoulders heaved up and down as she released her sorrow. Sorrow for her newborn son who was now out of her life, sorrow for the death of her cat and sorrow for herself for all she'd lost.

Elaine stood silently a few feet away watching her friend, who looked like a little lost and broken-down child, kneeling at the grave. She did her best not to break down and cry herself. Elaine had never liked cats, but Linda's cat had been unique—feisty and endearing. To visit Linda, meant also visiting Sweetie. It would be strange not to have him around anymore.

After giving her a few minutes alone, Elaine walked over and said, "He was a great cat."

Linda didn't immediately respond. Her bottom lip quivered as her eyes focused on Sweetie's resting place. "Oh Sweetie. My Sweetie. I'm so sorry. I love you, honey. Please wait for me in heaven and I'll join you soon." Linda sobbed uncontrollably as she reached out to stroke the earth.

"Yes, he was," Linda finally answered. "I just had to tell him goodbye." Grief covered her face as she slowly looked up. "Thanks, Elaine. Thanks for being such a good friend and thanks for bringing me here."

"No problem." Elaine quickly turned away, just in time to hide the tears that rolled down her own cheeks.

14
LOST

As the weeks slipped by, Linda no longer lived. She simply existed, numbed by all she'd experienced. She had quit the sales job immediately after Richard had let her down. She never wanted to see or hear from him again. Since then, she'd worked at temporary secretarial positions . . . up until Thanksgiving. After being released from the hospital, the last thing on her mind was to find a job: temporary or permanent.

Instead, she stayed in her dark apartment. She didn't watch TV, call anyone, or even answer the phone. She simply sat on the couch or out on her balcony next to Sweetie's daybed replaying the scenes of her son being taken away, the dogs attacking her and Sweetie dying over and over in her mind.

Late one afternoon Linda sat out on the balcony, looking at nothing in particular, when suddenly two large dogs came prancing into her line of vision. Terror swept over Linda. Once her pounding heart and racing pulse settled down, Linda stood, "I'm terrified of dogs! I can't let this one incident ruin my reaction to animals. I've got to do something constructive." Her mother's words from so long ago popped into her mind: *fall off a horse, climb right back on.* It was time for her to climb back on the proverbial horse.

She got up and walked inside with newfound energy. *What can I do to help me get over this terror of dogs?* She spotted the phone book and flipped through the pages.

That's it! Linda put her finger on the page, leaned over to pick up the phone and dialed the number.

A happy voice greeted her, "Animal Shelter, how can I help you?"

"Hi . . ." Linda began not knowing what she would say. "My name is Linda, and I want to volunteer to work with the animals."

"Well, that's great, Linda! We need volunteers. What kind of work are you interested in doing?"

"I'm not sure. What's available?"

The cheerful woman briefly explained some of the different types of positions before ending with, "You will need to come over to the shelter, fill out some forms, and go through an orientation before you can start. When you're here, you can decide which position sounds like the most fun for you." The woman paused. "I'm looking at the schedule and our next orientation is this Saturday morning. Can you make it?"

Linda glanced at her empty calendar. "Yes, I can."

She went to the orientation and learned in detail about the different positions but quickly realized she couldn't be in the shelter itself. It'd be too heart-wrenching if she became attached to an animal and it had to be put down. Her excitement about volunteering waned until the instructor mentioned the last option. "There is one last program we'd like to get started, but we haven't had anyone interested because it involves a lot of work." Linda listened intently. "It requires strong organizational and people skills, a love of animals *and* senior citizens plus local travel. Would anyone like to learn more about this?" Linda shot her hand up. Hers was the only one. "Great. Everyone else, please go ahead and fill out your paperwork, and you," the instructor said looking at Linda, "please, come with me."

Linda followed the instructor to a private office. "The program is called Pet-a-Pet," the woman said. "The idea behind it is to help seniors as well as the animals. Many of the senior citizens relinquished their pets before moving into senior housing and miss them desperately. Some may be angry, some sad. By bringing these homeless animals to them, the goal is to bring happiness to both the people and the animals. Does this sound like something you'd be interested in doing?"

"Yes!"

"Okay, well, there's more. It requires contacting retirement and nursing facility administrators to schedule visits, coordinating animal check-outs from the shelter, transporting the animals back and forth using your vehicle, maintaining control of the animals at all times, and lastly, you must conduct yourself as a professional representative of the shelter." The woman stopped and looked at Linda. "Are you still interested?"

In Linda's mind, it was a win-win-win situation. The animals got out of their cages, the seniors got to cuddle some pets, if only for awhile, and she'd only be handling cats and small dogs until she overcame her fear of large dogs. Linda didn't hesitate. "YES! I've been told I'm exceptionally organized, I love animals and people, and bringing smiles to others, gives me joy. When can I start?"

The lady chuckled. "As soon as you fill out this paperwork," she scooted a packet of papers toward Linda, "and we run a background check."

The following Saturday, Linda became the new Pet-a-Pet coordinator. Working with the animals got her out of the apartment, reconnected to other people and helped ease the pain of losing Sweetie. Over the next several months, she also overcame her fright of large dogs and severe depression. She started living again.

15
REUNITED

Linda finally got to see her son again in July. The adoption caseworkers had arranged for everyone to meet at a mutually "safe" ground—the office. Linda wondered what they were worried about . . . but didn't dwell on it. She just wanted to see her son again.

She arrived first. Aimee was on vacation that week, so Pearl led her down the hall to a room with white walls and beige carpeting, and told her to have a seat as she pointed at two couches placed against the walls. As Linda sat on one of the couches and waited, questions raced through her mind: *Did she look okay? Would her son's adoptive parents like her? Would she like them? Would her child remember her voice?*

All of Linda's thoughts ceased when the door opened. A tall woman with blonde hair and kind green eyes walked into the room. A man of about the same height with dark hair and black glasses followed her. He held Christian in his arms.

The woman walked right up to Linda. "Hi, my name is Lori." She wrapped her arms around Linda and gave her a huge squeeze. As Linda returned the hug, Lori whispered

Darkest Dawn

in her ear, "Thank you so much for the greatest gift possible. Thank you."

A huge lump suddenly blocked Linda's throat. She could not speak, so simply nodded her acknowledgement.

Lori stepped back and introduced her husband, Paul, who extended his hand to Linda. She shook it and then they sat down together on one sofa.

After a few moments of small talk, Paul asked Linda if she'd like to hold the baby. "Of course I would!" she said reaching for her son.

"We renamed him," Paul told her. "We call him David."

"I figured you would. I wrote him a big long letter telling him the name I chose for him but I also told him that it'd probably be changed."

"And, what a letter!" Lori said. "That letter had me in tears. I know David will appreciate it and your honesty, once he gets old enough."

"I hope so."

"He will!" Paul said. "It's very special and I'm sure not many birthmothers go to the trouble to share so much with their babies."

Not knowing what to say, Linda just smiled while looking down at little David.

After a brief silence, both Lori and Linda started to speak at once and then laughed at their timing. "You first," Lori said.

"Okay, thanks. I just have so many questions for both of you. Questions like when and how are you going to tell David about me. How often would you like to get together, all kinds of questions, but the biggest one is . . . I have a request."

Paul and Lori looked at her.

67

Linda looked down at the little boy in her arms then took a deep breath for courage and said, "I was wondering . . . it's just that Thanksgiving is so hard for me. It falls around the time my mom died, now around Chris—I mean David's birth and it's also when my cat died. It's such a hard holiday for me." She paused. "I was wondering if you could find it in your hearts to let me visit you on Thanksgiving to celebrate David's birthday with you?" Linda held her breath in anticipation. *What if they said no?* She waited with wide eyes glancing back and forth between them. Lori and Paul looked at each other and laughed.

"What?"

"That was one of the questions we were going to ask you, Linda," Lori said. "We thought it'd be the best day of the year for all of us to get together. Without you, we wouldn't have such a birthday to celebrate!"

"Oh thank you!"

The hour together passed quickly as Linda, Lori and Paul got to know each other better and marveled over their precious son.

The door to the room opened and Pearl peeked her head in. "I hate to break it up, but it's time to go."

"So soon?" asked Linda.

Pearl nodded. "Sorry! But it looks to me like you had a great visit."

In unison, Linda, Lori and Paul said, "We did!"

"Good! I'll give you a moment to say your goodbyes." Pearl stepped out and closed the door behind her.

In a flurry, Linda and Lori exchanged phone numbers and addresses. Linda gave her son one last tremendous squeeze before handing him back to Paul.

"You know," Lori said, "it's weird. I don't know how to explain it . . . but it's like we've already known each other for years!"

Linda agreed as they all walked out of the room together.

16
HOME

A year had passed since the darkest dawn of Linda's life. It was another sun-filled, warm November morning as she parked her same old—but trusty—car in the driveway filled with other vehicles. Before she got out, she admired the large white brick home with lots of windows and a lushly landscaped front yard. When she stepped out of the car, she noticed the view of the golf course just beyond the back yard. Linda took a deep breath to calm her nervousness, and then walked up to the front door. She heard laughter inside and smiled as she pushed the doorbell.

Almost immediately, Paul opened the door. A smile lit up his face as he greeted her. "You made it! We're so happy you could join us for Thanksgiving." Paul stepped back and waved her in.

Linda entered and looked around the entry hall. The large area had dark wood flooring, tan colored textured material on the walls and a large gold and glass chandelier hanging from the ceiling.

"Everyone is here and exited to see you . . . including Lori's parents." Paul led Linda through the dining room overlooking the golf course's second hole. A huge oak table held a stack of china plates and expensive silverware for the upcoming meal. They continued on to the family room, a warm, inviting area surrounded by light-colored paneled walls with three large comfy chairs and a love seat facing the room's fireplace.

As they entered the room, Paul said, "Look who's here!"

Laughter filled the room along with an overwhelming feeling of affection. Linda felt as if she had come home, at last.

Lori held the baby in her arms and walked up to Linda and Paul. With her free arm, she gave Linda a big hug, then led her down the one step into the family room and toward her parents. "Mom, Dad," Lori said, "this is Linda—David's birthmother."

Lori's parents came over to welcome Linda. Lori's mother reached out and touched Linda's shoulder, "Our grandson is our biggest blessing. Thank you."

Then Lori's father put his arm around Linda. "We want you to feel at home."

Paul walked over to the love seat and patted the cushion. "Come sit down, Linda."

Lori sat down next to Linda. "Would you like to hold David?"

Linda looked into her green eyes. "I'd love to!"

Lori handed her the squirming boy. Linda stroked his cheek, and the baby grabbed her finger, and then tried putting it into his mouth. Everyone laughed.

"Seems he's ready for Thanksgiving Dinner!" Linda said.

Lori handed her some Cheerios. "Here give him some of these. He loves them."

"Well, let's all sit down and get to know each other better," Paul said. Linda remained seated on the love seat, holding her son who was now tugging on her hair. Lori and her mother sat in the other chairs so they could watch Linda and David. "What have you been doing since we last saw you, Linda?" asked Paul.

Over the next hour everyone shared stories and Linda told the group about the volunteer work she loved as the Pet-a-Pet coordinator and about her new paralegal job. Everyone congratulated her.

Linda looked down at the baby in her arms, registering in her mind every little detail about him. He was truly precious. Then Linda looked over at Lori, then back at Paul and Lori's parents.

"Thank you to *all* of you for inviting me into your home for Thanksgiving and David's birthday. You just don't know how much this means to me to be here."

Lori looked toward Paul and then at her parents. They all smiled—as if in cahoots—at one another.

"Linda, you're invited for every Thanksgiving," Lori said as she sat next to her on the love seat, "and any time . . . because you *are* family. You're an important part of this family. Without you, we wouldn't have our son."

"And grandson!" Lori's mother added.

Paul joined in. "Linda, you are a member of this family . . . forever!"

The love she felt moved her to tears and she couldn't stop them as they spilt over her lashes. Linda hadn't been this happy since she was a child. She had finally found peace.

Carefully cradling the infant in her arms, Linda leaned over and gave Lori a hug with her free arm. Paul and Lori's parents walked over to get their hugs as well.

Lori's father, who had been standing behind the love seat, cleared his throat. "That turkey is calling me. I'll go get it sliced up so we can eat!"

"Sounds good," Lori's mother said. "I'll help you." Lori's parents walked into the dining room, arm-in-arm.

Soon a golden-brown turkey, platters filled with cranberry sauce, potatoes, gravy, green beans, pies and breads covered the table. Linda looked at all the food in awe. *This sure beats last year's meal of a bologna sandwich.*

As they began taking their seats, Paul said, "Wait a minute. I'll be right back."

Paul came back into the room with a camera and a tripod. He set up the equipment then instructed everyone to stand up and get close. Linda stood in the middle holding David in her arms, with Lori and Paul on each side and Lori's parents standing behind her. The camera's flash went off.

Paul ran back to the camera and repeated the process a couple more times. "Out of all those, I'm sure there's a great photo! Linda, I'll send you two copies . . . one for you and one for your caseworker's collection."

Linda remembered the photographs in Aimee's office on her shelves and desk. Now her happy story would be shared there as well. "Thank you so much! Happy Thanksgiving everyone and," she gently kissed the forehead of the baby, "Happy Birthday, David!"

The End

ೞೞಱ

ABOUT THE AUTHOR

Bonny Brookes lives in the hill country of central Texas.

Inspired by the gorgeous vista of hills, water and daily sunsets, she writes inspirational stories hoping to help others overcome adversity and insurmountable odds.

When not writing or doing volunteer work with animals, she cuddles with her finicky felines, travels, plays piano or guitar, reads and photographs nature and wildlife.

www.ingramcontent.com/pod-product-compliance
Lightning Source LLC
Chambersburg PA
CBHW031330040426
42443CB00005B/278